A Day in the Life Of A Worm

Ruby Tuesday Books

Ruth Owen

Little Acorns

Published in 2025 by Ruby Tuesday Books Ltd.

Editor: Mark J. Sachner
Design: Tammy West
Production: John Lingham

Photo Credits:
Alamy: 9 (Auscape International), 14 (pq pictures), 15 (Zuma Press Inc); Dreamstime: 7 (Razvan Cornel Constantin); Dwight Kuhn: 11, 12T, 19; Nature Picture Library: 10 (Laurent Geslin), 17 (Solvin Zankl); Shutterstock: Cover (MakroBetz), 4T (Alexander Raths), 5 (D. Kucharski K. Kucharska), 6 (golf bress), 8 (Eviart), 12B (AliaksaB), 13 (neenawat khenyothaa), 18T (Tomasz Klejdysz), 18B (schankz), 20T (Peter Kniez), 20B (Wirestock Creators), 21T (Evan Lorne), 21B (Serhii Ivashchuk), 22 (GTW, kungfu01, & Kaca Skokanova), 23 (Majna, Ayman Haykal, Tama2u, & krolya25), 24 (Tob1900).

Library of Congress Control Number: 2024941218

Print (Hardback) ISBN 978-1-78856-507-3
Print (Paperback) ISBN 978-1-78856-508-0
ePub ISBN 978-1-78856-509-7

Published in Minneapolis, MN
Printed in the United States

www.rubytuesdaybooks.com

CONTENTS

It's Cool Underground!

It's a hot, sunny day in a backyard.

But in an earthworm's underground world, it's always dark, damp, and cool.

If the worm's skin gets dry, it will die!

So it keeps out of the hot sun.

The worm's body is soft, but it can push through solid soil.

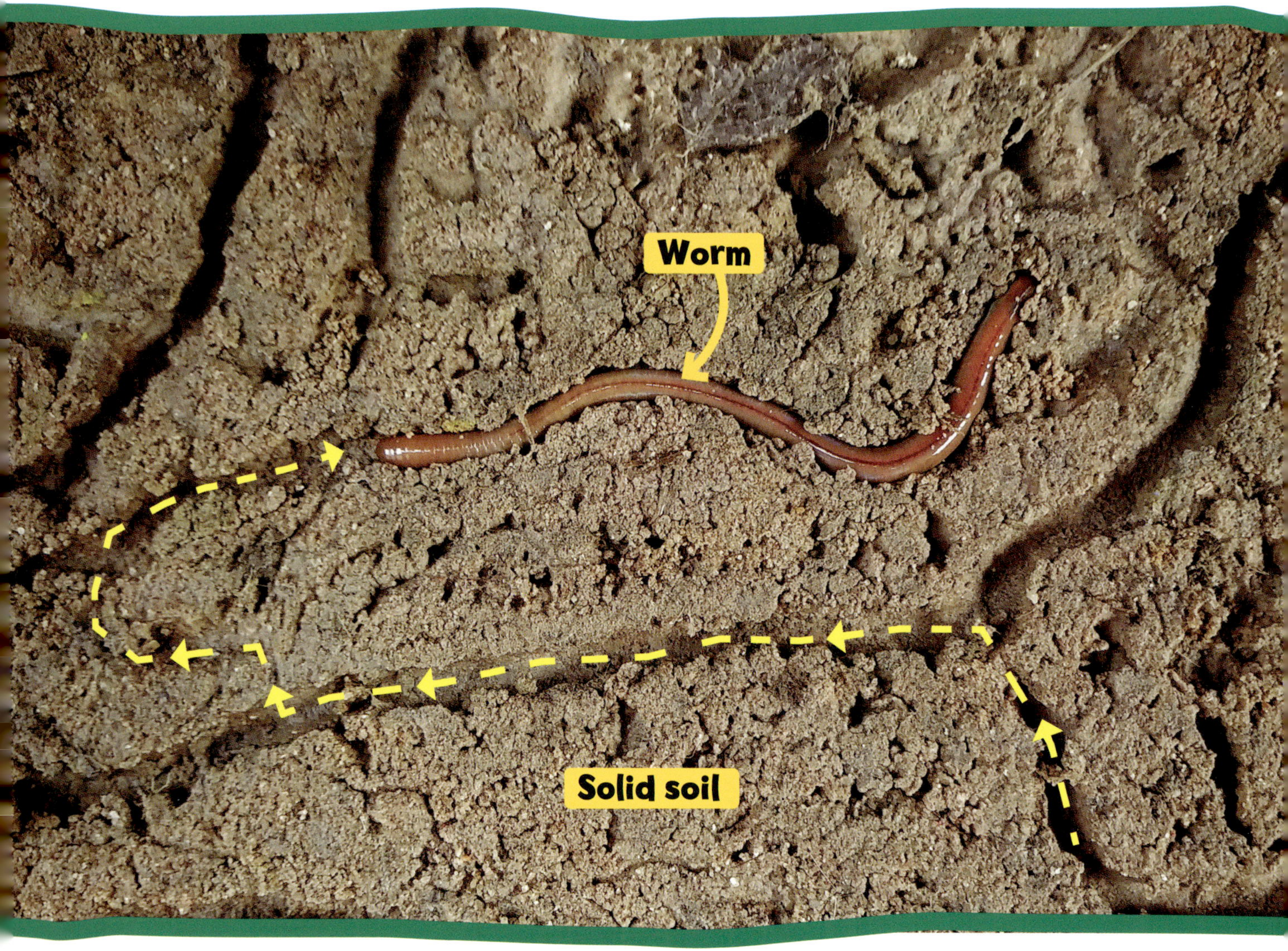

It has hair-like **bristles** on its skin.

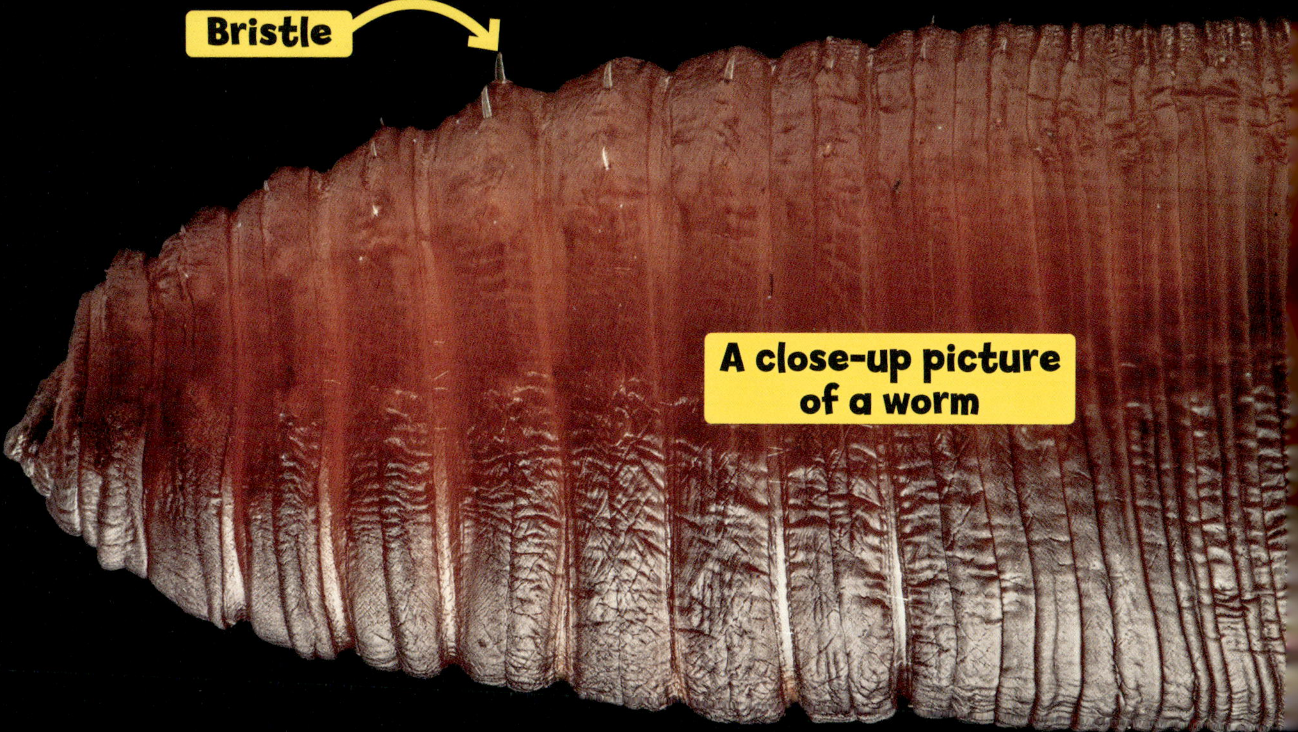

The bristles help the worm push forward.

The worm is very helpful to the backyard plants. How?

Worms make little holes and tunnels in the soil.

Rainwater trickles through the holes and tunnels.

This helps water get to the roots of plants.

Grass plants
Plant roots
Worm hole
Worm in tunnel

When evening comes, the worm wriggles from its underground world.

It's time to find food!

The worm eats **rotting** leaves.

Worms help clean up dead plants.

The worm eats rotting fruit and vegetables.

A rotting pumpkin

The worm makes poop called castings.

The castings become part of the soil, and help feed plants.

When morning comes, the worm wriggles back into the soil.

But a hungry bird grabs the worm's tail!

The bird pulls

and pulls

and pulls.

The worm's bristles hold on tight to the soil.

BOING!

The bird lets go, and the worm gets away.

But there are hungry **predators** underground, too.

A mole is hunting for worms in the soil.

Just in time, the worm gets away!

Today, the worm makes a **cocoon**.

There are eggs inside.

A baby worm hatches from each egg.

It wriggles from the cocoon.

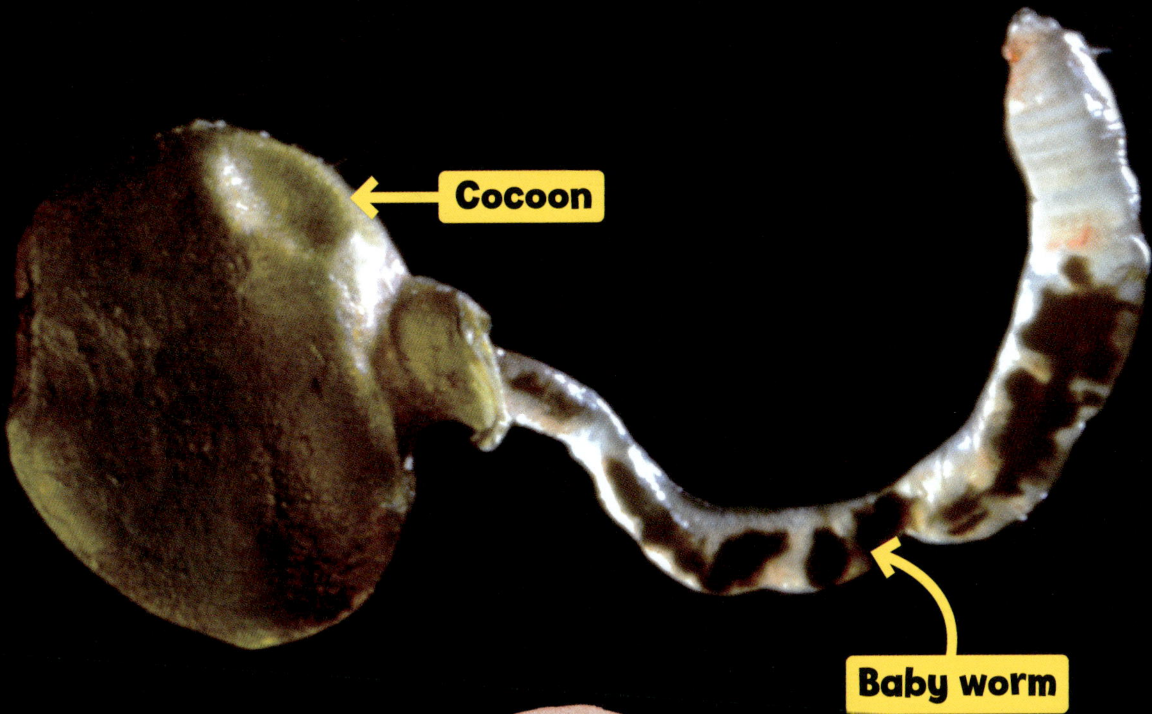

A worm **mates** with another worm before making eggs.

Suddenly, the worm's underground world is moving and shaking!

Up

Up

Up

Someone digs up the worm.

They put the worm on a **compost heap**.

Worms eat rotting stuff on a compost heap.

It's the perfect new home for a worm!

Glossary

bristle
A short, stiff hair on an animal or person's body.

cocoon
A covering that protects eggs or a young insect, such as a caterpillar.

compost heap
A box or heap of dead plants, old vegetables, eggshells, and other matter that rots and becomes new soil.

mate
To come together to produce young.

predator
An animal that hunts and eats other animals.

rotting
Breaking down and becoming moldy. Rotting leaves and fruits become part of the soil.

Index